Free Gifts Given to You Along the Way

ALICE LEGG

ISBN 978-1-64114-474-2 (paperback)
ISBN 978-1-64114-475-9 (digital)

Copyright © 2018 by Alice Legg

All rights reserved. No part of this publication may be reproduced, distributed, or transmitted in any form or by any means, including photocopying, recording, or other electronic or mechanical methods without the prior written permission of the publisher. For permission requests, solicit the publisher via the address below.

Christian Faith Publishing, Inc.
832 Park Avenue
Meadville, PA 16335
www.christianfaithpublishing.com

Printed in the United States of America

In Memory of Angela and Cherie

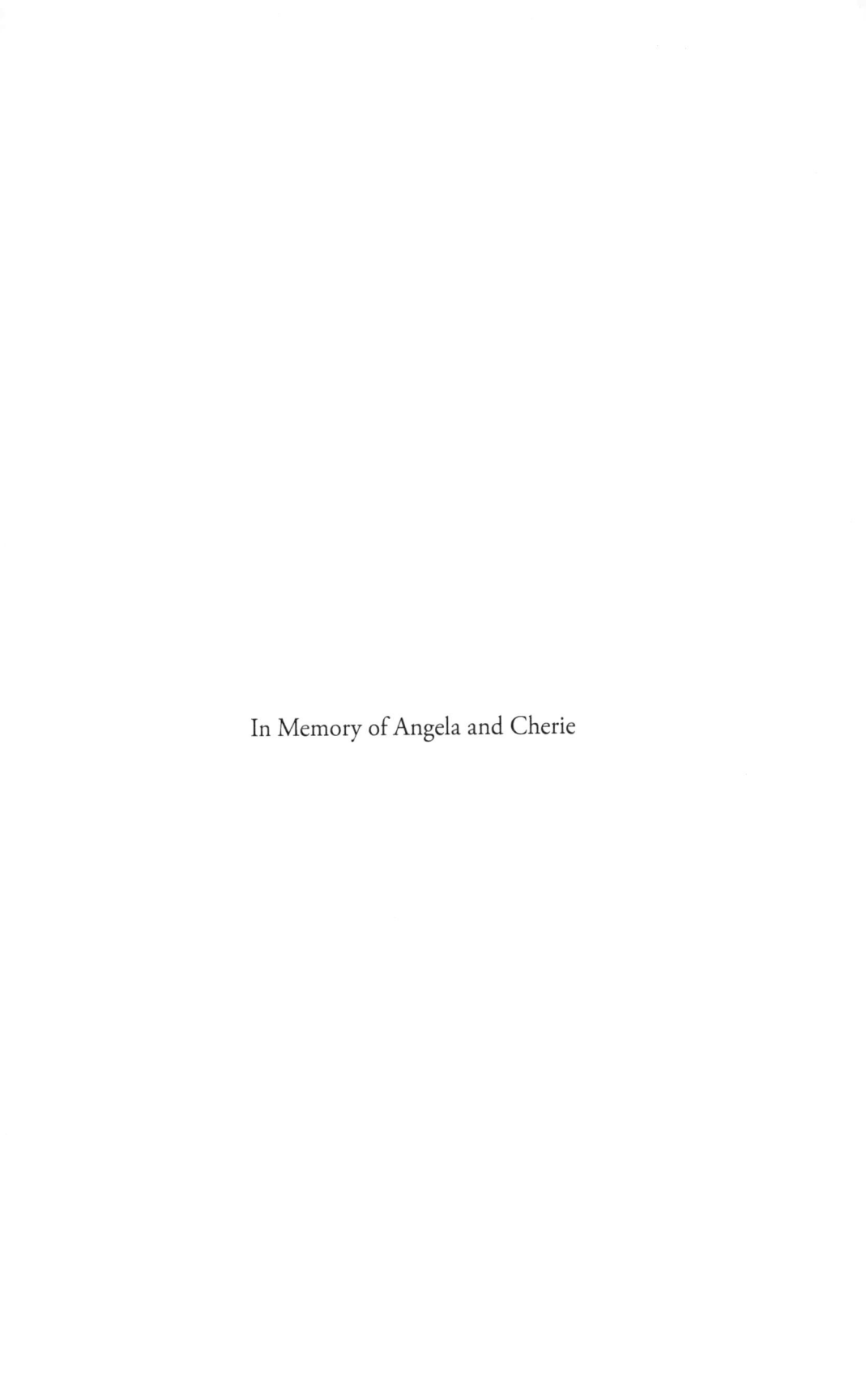

You

You are one in millions God made
That God gave life
Only you he had in mind
He made you a certain way this day
To serve him and love him in every
Way seek and find the price
Was paid for all the cross he's
Not willing for anyone lost
The son of God shows the way offers
This every day and way

Dream

Was it a dream was it real the
unseen present that I feel it's
Here at the door again and asked
Please let me in to come into
your heart and forgive you
of all sin when you asked
from beginning to the end
I want to do this just for
You to let you know I love you

The Cat

My Cat always there I come
Home she meets at the door
She's my pet I knew she was mine
The time I met her on the
Street hungry and cold I fed her
Right away I opened the door and let
Her in sometimes she seems to
Stare at me as if to say thank
You ever so much I think I'll
Stay long time she my friend
Until she out sick and went to
Heaven that day animals are there
Too you feel it when you are
Blue there's animals in
Heaven too

Light Dark Time

Day and night times goes on not
To stay where it went where it is
Something we can't get back
Up in heaven, no time, no end
He sent the time for us to use
He gives maybe more maybe less
I don't know I couldn't guess

Thank You

Thank you for the things I cannot do
All for all the things you give me.
Help, Lord, clear the way
Ahead because I believe
All words you said
Thank you over and over
Again, for forgiveness for my sin.

The Stamp

All shapes, sizes, too pay a
Little or a lot
Put me in the corner of the envelope
Put in the love letter you wrote
To travel there and back to me
A stamp you will need.
To let me know let me learn
Your love letter to me
Our love to confirm.

Are You

Are you the one to come and
Heed the call
To pass God's word on give the news
The old story we hear far away and near.
Good news not bad makes you
Happy but not sad
Away there without a doubt don't
Keep it in let it out
For good news is hard to find
News that you will ever hear
Someone loves them, love them
That is clear.

ABC

Letters we need to read and write
Just some of them there are more
My favorite ones are
Jesus for I think they
Are the best
Name is forever what it means
Only one, one of a kind
Keeps us in mine
Rain or shine.

Yes or No

Yes or no? Makeup your mind
Do we agree or disagree?
Let's talk some more to make you see
Stay together not apart so we
can make a brand new start.

Days

Take the days slow and live
the way you should.
Remember to do as the Lord would
do and it will always come back
to you and more,
because you took the time to
be kind, caring, and more
Look through the opened door go through
because God has helped you.

Songs

Sing the songs of praise because
the Lord he did raise
he did so we would live
if we choose if not we will
lose; listen, listen heed the call
He gave this freely to us all
on this earth, His son was here
Sing the songs of good cheer

Bunnies

Bunnies, their floppy ears,
Their little nose
Four little feet go
Hop, hop, hop,
they are like this us in a way but
cannot say
Don't have the needs people do not like me and you
but I'm sure they will also be
there in the sky when they
die, it just makes sense that
they're God's creation too
like me and you

Mom and Dad

Not easy growing up not a lot
you had lots of kids I would
think you did the best you could
Take a message sent
By the wind from Here to There
A word for you to hear
the both of you I love you, dear.

Eyes

Eyes to see tell a lot look around
you read and more.
Sometimes seems like they can talk
Look deep into the eyes they tell a lot
see problems they do tell you lot more.
What they hide and don't let out
but keep inside.

Arms

Arms we use every day for so
many things we need
A hug for someone to let them
know you care.
Don't wait till they are not here
let them know how you feel,
care your concern
Just in case they don't return.

Sun

A glowing ball in the sky above our head
Keeps us warm when we are cold
Helps us grow our food
You feel the sun the people
say it's going to be a new day
If I could put in a bottle for
a rainy day, just escape, and go away
No one can for it's meant to
Shine not mine I can't keep
nature is for us to use enjoy was
meant everything the Lord has sent.

Love

As you walk along the path of life
Iam there I watch you sleep through the night
look inside, open your heart, I am there in all
the days of your life beginning to end I
never leave you or let you down, yet you never talk
to me, I am here, look around everything that is
beautiful I made for you all life's trials I am
There listen to your inner voice talk to me
I am in your mind and thoughts I share
Trust me call on me talk to me anytime
I care I am love.

The Cat

My cat always there I come
Home she meets at the door
She's my pet I knew she was mine
The time I met her on the
Street hungry and cold I fed her
Right away opened the door and let her in
Sometimes she seems to
stare at me as if to say thank
you ever so much I think I'll
stay long time she my friend until she got sick and went to
Heaven that day animals are there
Too you feel it when you are
Blue there are animals in
Heaven too

Light Dark Time

Day and night times goes on not
To stay where it went where it is
Something we can't get back
up in Heaven no time no end
he sent the time for us to use
he gives maybe more maybe less
I don't know I couldn't guess

You

You are one in millions; God made that, God gave life
Only you he had in mind
He made you a certain way this day
To serve him and love him in every
Way to seek and find the price
Was paid for all the cross he's
not willing for anymore lost the son
of God shows the way offers this
every day and way

Dream

Was it a dream or was it real?
Unseen present that I feel.
It's here at the door again and asked
please let me in, to come into
your heart and forgive you
of all sin.
When you asked
from beginning to the end
I want to do this just for you
to let you know, I love you

The Candle

Light spread the light warm
the heart to someone in need
out of sight.
Come out, come out, listen to me
I'm the one who does care
I'm there
But best of all, I'm everywhere.

Thorns

A crown of thorns was on his head
the words he heard so unkind
up the road he did tread
and to die as he said
but what he offers us doesn't hurt
the trumpets sound here them roar
and blow
the crown he offers is pure gold.

People

I watch people as they walk by sometimes a
Lot, sometimes none. Stop, I am here
What is life that's not clear I am
hungry and want some food
a place to stay another day help
each other as the Lord would do, I cry,
please don't pass me by.

The Chair

I can't get up to walk out of this chair
to walk anywhere.
But in my mind, I can go there I
can go anywhere.
Keep in mind you can walk again
by his wounds he suffered so
for all of us to heal.
Pray believe healing is real
I can get up and walk again
it's time because the Lord did say
and still happens even today

Zoo

Bear they stare to let us know to beware
Elephant I like their trunk as they pick up the logs to clear the way to build our home today
Giraffe has long neck to pick the leaves way up high, he like them the most of all, he can get them because he's tall
Horse, of course, he won the race you bet on; take care of him he likes hay to go and win for you another day; there are so many in the zoo can't speak for them all, small, large, some small.

Water

Bottled or from the tap we drink
All the flavors all kinds for you to choose and to see
Water also keeps and clean
Both shower cold hot
Take it early take it late
it also cooked the food we ate
so many things it will do good for you
God sent for us to use
needed can't go without
God knows our needs without a doubt

Free

Free as a bird I can fly because I'm in heaven thatis why. I decided to keep his word and the Lord to seek. I followed him to the end because he forgave me of all sin I did, did escape; and now, I see Heaven's gate.

Christmas New

Happy birthday. This is the day God sent you to us to say. But I will come another day unseen. But always there to hear your every prayer. Here, the book, read it well just to keep it gives all the information you will need to go on life's way. Here, take it today.

Powerful

The Angels look down into the pit the evil covers and hides its face. I am the most powerful. I tell you again and again. Believe, I tell you, this day, I overcome today anything that comes your way.

Thinking

Knowing things, there is a limit to what is above the clouds higher to end he leaves us with things we do not. Know so at the end he will show us at life's end. The wonders of the land he leaves all of this, he gives forevermore nothing like it anywhere; believe it, he does care!

Oceans

Deep, Deep Ocean doesn't know what I will find when you are the pirates' ship. Ho, ho, ho, just might find a pot of gold. Would be nice if it was gold until you look you will never know.

The Golden Hen

In a number ten
One she laid the egg
Two I ate it for breakfast and I said
Three she worked so hard for me
Four I was good should have some more two or three
Five I'm glad she's alive
Six the food I give to her I mix
Seven to eat seven maybe eleven
Eight check time can't be late
Nine I keep her she's so kind
Ten I win what pair life good
the pets your share
and if that's case she would be an ace.

Me

I am the one you are looking for
great gifts I have in my store
come let's go and shop
for the things only in this store
Can't buy offers free that is
Why for you to come to me
I give life you see
So, come go shop will you or will you not.

The Ride

Up the road not always smooth
there are bumps and hills too
Country town where are you bound
and if your ride should quit
open your heart of love pour it in and it will start again.
And if you give someone a ride
Where he goes he does not know
show him where you are going
And he can too, the talk we had
Helped him more then he could say
Thank you! Thank you! Have a nice day!
Open up and pour more in
another journey to begin

Healing Hands

The love so much you are well
Just a touch if you believe this
can be give it a try and you will see.
I could not, but I can
But know his words are true,
his words for all of you brand new.

World

World of wonder, I can see
Ocean to ocean, sea to sea,
Hills and valleys, mountain tops,
more, more, lots and lots
A world that God had made
To Heed his call he made us all
and to go follow him to
the world where's there is no end.

Flowers

Every color every shape a
seed planted and it will grow
from the soil you put it
in to sow to look at or
pick it put it in a vase somewhere
in your special place
Soon they will grow again
Just one of the pleasures God did send.

Sand

Walk in the sand it makes
A mark where it starts where
It ends the footprints I see
In mind reminds me the
Lord was there for me every
Time every day his always there makes a way.

Life

Life goes on, but it will end seems slow
But really fast but for
Everyone it will end someday
Look in the mirror I am
Young, but again I am old, be
Ready ask forgiveness for your sin
To go to the place where you will live again

Fire

See the glow don't touch it
Will burn hot, hot warm we
Need for things to day fire is
Not for play I told you time and
Time again don't touch it will
Burn you did not listen to me
Now you hurt you see.

Tea Bags

Boil the water put in your cup
Soak me good to your taste
Mix lemon, sugar milk, or all
Let me stay till I blend ok
To perk you up to start your
Day or coffee you may want
Brew me up in the pot coffee
Also helps me a lot.

Shapes

Small, large, round, and square more
Shapes that form as a picture
I begin paint it, color it, I don't
Know for sure what I am trying
To show but if I keep doing my work
I see and show the thing I want you to know
when it's done I show it to you to see
It's a picture of you and me

Go and come

Go to work and back home other place too.
Time you need to travel these
Traffic slow to go we need
Time for us and all the rest too
As you go and come do the right
Thing someone out there you
Could help too as they travel
The same as you do too

Books

Books are good, real, fake, I read
But the one that helps the most.
And its true help is the one upon the shelf.
take it down and dust if off read it
And you learn the way to go the way to turn.
On the bible pages the treasure you found.
The map so old that he wrote
All the words he spoke.

Sheep

We are like sheep come to the fold
If get lost here his call
Come back again.
Not just you all have sin
Go back again and mend the
Torn apart, get together again,
Not half, but whole.

Daughter

Newly created by God's hand
A few days the problems began
only a short time on this earth,
the breath of life from her did
go up to live again in the
mansions of Gold.
Hard to take hard to see
try and remember God knows
best for knows all he took
her to stay by his side this day
byday something to say that
might help the hurt that comes
Where you have lost loved ones.

Heaven

I wonder what it's like I know
There is a great light.
people there not like as they fly
And clear new you can see right through.
Pretty flours along the way and more
Steps that go back to Earth and
up again steps God did send
He alone only knows up there
Climb the stairs do his will
Wait till you one day you see
Heaven's gate to open for you and me

Empty

I search and search for something not
They're everywhere, all I do
Nothing will help I fear I'm lost I fall.
And he stands me on my feet.
The rest of my life him I seek,
Hope someday that we will meet
And forever his word I'll keep.

Don't Cry

Don't cry I will see you by and by.
Listen I tell you why the bible
tells us the Lord hears our cry
Lets us know we are safe you can go on your way note
I'm really ok!
Lord willing, we will see each other again one day.

The House

The house is a home people
a place to share they
go and come eat, talk, leave
through their day and more
they are welcome you wait
for their return this makes a
house a home you care
Home is home because you are there.

Pigs

Pigs they are so cute and sweet
their little not and curly tail
they are for sale for meat
but when you pet their little head.
The taste you had for pork
is gone away after you met
the little pig today.

Life

Life goes on it's so fast what's today is the past.
For some for me everyone will end.
Don't know where or when.
Ask, repent, get to know the word God has sent.
Questions answered now I'll see
What's in store God has for me.

Questions

I have I miss hard to explain
I am I am not.
The world offers a lot but it will all go away
Looking for something more.
Release peace I seek.
Answers to the question I have
I am weak, but you are strong
Answers given all day long.

The Gift

Has no bow or a box
sent from above to below no surprise.
But good news, don't lose, just win
because from heaven, God's son
The gift he sent for all
store in a special place
contains the keys that opens the golden gates.

The Stone

Very large the one that blocks
the way into the cave that day
until it moved away.
No one inside
The guards said this
cannot be we have been
tricked you see
search and search
that they did far and near
to find the man gone up
into the sky to meet us by and by.

The Collector

I collect, but not things old or
new but I collect you to
go up with me in the clouds of
blue I'll come again maybe soon
you know not when.
Come all come soon I ask and
ask for rooms I prepare because
I care, I care.

Too Late

Too late it's not you still have time I am not mean, but I am kind come ask me all is there for you to see look up not down listen to my call before you take the fall into the deep pray, pray my sole to keep.

Name

What is a name?
Where did it come from?
There are all kinds.
I don't know if I like mine.
It's just a word
Did you hear? Have you heard?
Lord Jesus is His name the only one
The same for all of us he took the blame

Long Day

What to do I am very blue
Don't want to do anything
Don't know what
The day will bring my strength is about gone
I just sit the day away I think it's good
To pray for he will help to go on, but not alone
I cried for he is a right by my side

Bees

They fly around sometimes up sometimes
Down and around if the honey you
Did take put a cover on beware?
Their home you break into and surely they will sting you
Oh, this tastes good I really know that it would.

The Mark

You do not want if you gave away
The freedom to pray and serve the Lord day by day
What was easy but now very *hard* you have to suffer and maybe die for
What you believe for the savior he did leave only to return
Who are ready to go just a promise his love to show

Seasons

Winter, summer, spring, and fall
We know them all they come again never end
Some like some perfect snow sun leaves or all no choice
enjoy or not, the place you live.
Move to get what you want and leave
Behind the sun shine or shine not
snow or not, go where you want
seasons come and go again
Sent by God not by men.

Children

They are honest and kind trusting you
a perfect person God has sent to you
as they grow they have to be told
it's sad, people are good, people are bad
be careful and be aware, listen, take care
for in this world this is so
say yes or no how they live where to go
right, wrong, the Lord Helps
whatever will come their way.

The Wedding

Yes, yes, I do, I do the cake cut with a knife
You are now husband and wife,
don't go astray be true just because I love you
Two hearts blend together make one
Two or more may come a son or a daughter
Or more blessed by God we are thankful for
Our love to last forevermore.

Money

Money is nice we need to have
Only there are some things it cannot buy
Life, health, happiness are some
No matter how much you have to save
To save yourself you cannot do
Ask, receive, it's free
Never to end
Because his son he did send

All for Me

He carried the cross made from a tree
Just so I would not be lost,
Freely he gave his life he could have said no
He would go upon the hill the cross and die
he did this for me and you
True, true I know the word has told me so.

XXO

A game we play maybe win, maybe loose
It's a choice we have to choose
but if you do it right you will be ok
and sleep the night the new day
comes the sun will shine
problems will arise there will be some
but real not a game
God's son the same, the same.

True

Pass it on all you can all
Threw out the land
The man you will know him by his scars
Upon his hands feet and side
The holes that go right through
I don't know if you knew he did
This for you and me can't you see no one else
Would do he love you.

The Cake

The cake is like us in a way
it could rise, it could fall, get up, and try again
Ask for help God gave all men
make it again just rises don't fall
stay true one day he will come for all
Thru the clouds, thru the blue
All of this he will do
Not for just me or two
But for all of you
Take the road the right way
Listen to God's word what he has to say.

Rain

Rain upon my face I want to go to a safe place
As I walk along the road I see a church
Why I went in I don't know why
Maybe just to keep me dry
The man in front asked me to stay
The message he did say
The tears did come my face wet again
As I asked for forgiveness for my sin

Prison

Now I'm in my mistake
Put me here family can't be near
Short visits and they will go
Time to think about what I done
It was wrong I really know
Because the bible tells me so
Until at last my ways I mend
Never to do again
Wait, wait, time so slow
Until one day they let me go.

My Dog

She like cats I don't know about rats
The knock at the door she lets me know
Hoping for a friend not a foe
She loves attention people, food, and toys
I take her for a walk and play
She goes to bed what a pal
She gives back to people's needs cares,
She is small acts tall comes when I call
All the things she does for me.
I will keep her don't you see
All pets need a home - go out
And get your own

My Guy

You are like the rainbow
I see in the skies
The deep blue of your eyes
Helps me I care for you
You are there and true
That is why I love you.

Talk

Talk to me my Heart is broken
And I fear let me know are you here
The voice that comes with in your heart
Quiet, listen, let it start
Hard to explain answers just you will know
Just because he loves you so
Faith, believe the answer will come
Nothing impossible, nothing too hard
The Angels watch the mighty power of his great hands.

Eyes

Human eyes see only what they can
Pain sickness all you can bear
Just remember God is there
He decides just one touch
He doesn't allow it to be too much
Seeing all he has a plan for all
He hears us when we pray decides
Do we go, do we stay
Yes, no, we don't understand
He alone we can trust no less
He always knows what's best

Directions

Hear the wind see the sky
Earth all the trees, water flows by
God created for all to share
The birds the animals what a wonder too
But most of all he created you
Special in all ways he loves you
Cares for you, all your days
The cross there stands a sign
The way to go for all mankind

Love

No greater a love for you than God son has
The pain died for you rose lived again
No one could care so much
As he gave his life for us
No other way to say God gives us everyday
The road we walk until we see
Heaven's gate the light
Then we know we won the fight
The price only he would give for us to forever live.

Alone

No way just kneel and pray
Feel his present by your side
Day by day he will never go away
If you have no one else only one
He will always care to the very last day
He is there, just pray, believe the word and lives
The way he commands
He will make the footprints in the sands
He carries you when you are weak
When on your knees the Lord you seek

Heaven

Look at the flowers along the streets of gold
What a wonder for eyes behold
The animals are there too
Love ones come running to meet you
Crystal clear, but you know
Because your heart tells you so
The power of a mighty God
No more on Earth to trod free be with God

Church

Thinking of your love ones lost
their smiling faces look down on you
The word of God to share
As you take your seat
One day you all shall meet
Feel their present as if to say
I'm with God and I'm ok
Be of good cheer I'm glad
You are here in church today

Forgive

One life they took their own questions
No answers why
Wonder where they went
We were not there and don't know
What prayer was said?
Because I chose not to live
Time min's just a few
Lord I pray forgive me too.

Special

Look at me I cannot walk
Or maybe even talk or see
I'm a person too only
I wasn't born like you
Just love, don't hate
Reach out and help me along the way
You will receive it back one day
Thank you so much for showing you care
I thank God you were there

Quiet

I feel a present sight unseen
Knowing in your mind
This must be the one who created all mankind
Knowing there is hope for all your problems
To be solved this present
That I feel is here, saying don't fear
Because I love you dear
It's just me you feel
I'll stay and never, never go away
You opened your door and let me in
And let me forgive of all sin

Look

Look up the picture that I took of the sky above
The trees, the clouds that form I think
I see great arms that hold the angels
High a face, a dog, a man that wears the hat
Walking away into the blue
A baby in a cradle too
I see in the sky of blue
For me this is true

Read

Hoping someone will read
Some way will help their need
Knowing this is the only way
And they will seek their God today

Turtle

Slow turtle tries to win the race
Others faster go right by sure they
will win get off the track go astray
The turtle knows if he keeps going forward
Don't stop see the signs
Stay in the lines he be first to cross the finish line
Slow follow rules don't give up
Like the turtle stay in you will be a winner in the end.

Sorry

Sorry for what I did to you
What is it that I can do to?
Let you know I didn't mean to hurt you
If I could change it I would
Surely do give me a chance
Forgive me too I want to stay
With you because I still love you

Needle

Thread the needle, sew away
Mend the tear in my heart today
The needle I can't find
I know not how or what to do
The Lord could see and looked right through
He knows the way to mend me and you.

Rescue

If only I had done what was right to do
and did not turn and go the other way.
I would not be in this place with all the problems now I face
If only now past is past
The future doesn't have to be the same
I can make the change in me
A new me that is free
The Lord did see me when I asked
He came and rescued me at last

Pain

A child cannot say but believe
What we see with our human eyes
Isn't always there
We learn a know the touch
God didn't allow it to be too much
They did no wrong don't understand
Everything this man to stay there
By our side there, care, stay.
Know it in every way God did not go away

Because of Him

Because of him another day and a place to stay
Because of him the clothes I wear
A job and a way to get their food is on my plate I eat
With the water that I drink
My body and all its needs
Spirit too mine the sun the earth
Stop, think of all these things are worthy
But more seek my soul to save most of all meet
Surely all my needs he did give up we live.

Cat and Mouse

The cat that chased the mouse into the hole
He will hide there the cat cannot get for now safe
Put some cheese in the hole
then he comes out again to eat
the cat that didn't leave he waits
See the mouse begins the chase
The cat and mouse are not friends
The story the same
See each other play the game
Lots of fun until that day will
Come game is over game is done
The end

No

No, I don't agree because in Christ I believe
No, I will not change at all
It is true not false he died for all that are lost
Come here I will explain the news
So you will know you say you have not heard no one said a word
The best news yet I glad to let you know ask pray say yes
But *No* all he said he will do not false but true

Don't Know

If we have another day pray to God this is so
But we really don't know
If by God's grace He allows more time, more
Days, He will give his will.
Do you best, do your all
Know not when God will call for
us to be with him
Time run out can't escape it's for all
The time clock ticks away
until it stopped that one day

Snow

Snow reflects the light tonight to make it some more bright
But in the morning sun of day it will melt away.
Shovel, shovel, clear the way
I hope it doesn't snow no more today
My snowman that I built has
began to tilt and melt away it's gone.
The carrot I gave it for a nose.
I'll give to the dear that has been
Staring at me so clear when he thinks I'm not
looking that way he will
get the carrot and run away.

Merry Go Round

Listen to the music enjoy the sound
take a ride go round and round
Now it's time to get off
Step down take some time to think
Where I'm at the next step to take
To keep the things I have kept
or let go change start new
Think who I am go straight
not round and round
Why I'm here the purpose in my
life pray that I can help someone
one day a person I never knew or
even it could be you

Parents

Early morning so peaceful and slow
Make a list of what to do and where
to go and chores too
for the kids and you I'll fix
something to eat to go out to work
and school I need to hurry the day
won't last to do my many tasks
what is a day, I don't know, won't last
gone can't get back
I also forgot to ask you dad to mow the lawn.
I know this he will do
Because he also loves you too

Sandals

Sandals upon his feet he walked
the sands of the deserts deep
The staff that helped him stand up
Journeys long water food gone
Strength given from above
We are weak, but he is strong
Help sent to finish the task
for you and me
and what was meant to be.

Tests

Will you stand for what you believe?
Tests that will happen for you to take.
Question how will you score
not waiver stay one place
Keep your eyes upon the cross
not side to side, but straight in
this will be your guide
for he will be right by your side.

The Way

Any way here to stay until
he opened up the skies of
blue to return for you
the triumphs roar returned as
he said and to raise the dead.
Only to know what he wrote
and said sight unseen
okay, what did he mean
on him I will lean to see
the right unseen.

Toes

Toe on my feet I need them all
To keep my balance so I don't fall
Also, I could count on them
five and five are ten
the small one is my pinky toe
Color them red and make them glow.

Windows

Windows look thru inside outside
so many there which one is best
Better than all the rest. The window
to your heart could be why you see
soft not hard open and you will see
completely clear not a smear.

His Hands

He opened up the sea so the righteousness
people could flee He talked to
the man the burning bush
and a message sent on a stone
just a few miracles just some
There are many more to come.

Chains

Chains I was bound to go on heavy
Pain but don't see for me
I only I know there something
wrong something sad until
One day I just knew for me
ask the Lord to set me free
He broke the chains to from me
go to move around free of sin
what a joy! Life's begin

2017

What will bring the world today?
such a mess, more good things?
I guess bad things less
Things will happen the world
the Lord has said he would protect us from
all harm you will be there
not too late gives the way for our escape.

The Boat

How big it was built to take
the storm with all its guests
the Lord did send but not
completely for the world to end
and when the time had come
to see the rising sun
The branch, the bird's wings are dry
then the boat floats ashore
To begin the world to start once more.

Art

Different Things, different kinds
What do you prefer? Nature offers a lot
Trees, animals, there is a lot of things we did not make
But given to us Best artist from
beginnings to now but we just
Don't know how what the Lord created we could not do
just something to think about
the power that is there everywhere
You can find anywhere anytime

Wonder

Wonder or try to guess How
the world stays in place Sun
moon stars universe always stays in
place I thinkHow this could be
There must be someone we don't
see out there protecting you and
me. Answers for our problems
To no matter How Big they are
the answer that we choose
Believethe words written in
a Book long time ago you can
Read the words that say to you
Believe me I am true
The wonder you are looking to
has the answer for you too.

Today

Twenty-four hours as I live life I
don't know have to see life
is so stressful you and me.
What do I do to peace with
it all ask for Help that's all.
I need some Help for this Day
I think I will just pray
The best is yet to come I
believe for sure the lord does
have the cure
I don't Know Where else to turn
But count on Sure things from
above is there I know someone
I'm not alone but have all
The help I need because I
Asked the lord to lead

Better Times for Me

I guess we have to go need to eat and get
some food other things too
not like the days years ago when
people had their food to grow Hunt Trade
It's hard work not in a good mood don't like
I don't have money have to trade
A goat and a couple chickens too from me to you
Would you trade your horse to me
The goat for some milk eggs from
The chicken too just for you
I need the horse to pull my wagon
to go to town too far to walk ok
What a relief I can ride to Town
to Shop and trade for what else I need
on my way don't forget to get the
hay to of course need this for
My new House
Home, Home, I go it's almost dusk
dark tomorrow to start the same again
All the supplies God gave
And strength to do my Chores
In the future as things progress not as
Hard work less

Where Did It Go?

The bucket I poured water in
I wonder why I could not fill
Where it went I looked and my bucket had
a hole in it
I wonder why I could not save
on bills, it all went.
Some things you have some things just go.
But one thing does not leave or go
Is the love Jesus offers you to keep
He tells you how to save and always
Have free will and to ask find out.
Talk to him pray what is it all about.
The bucket will always be full
hole or not
The money that you spent will
Multiply
God takes care of us that's why.

Give

Give me this, give me that all the time
you can't have because its mine if you
Keep it all someday it could be your
downfall. Now I have all this stuff
Have it all where to put it Have too much
Have enough for more than one
Oh, I think I changed my mind I don't
need it all give out take it all for me
Let someone else have some you see
I will be alright you see
After all God gave it to me

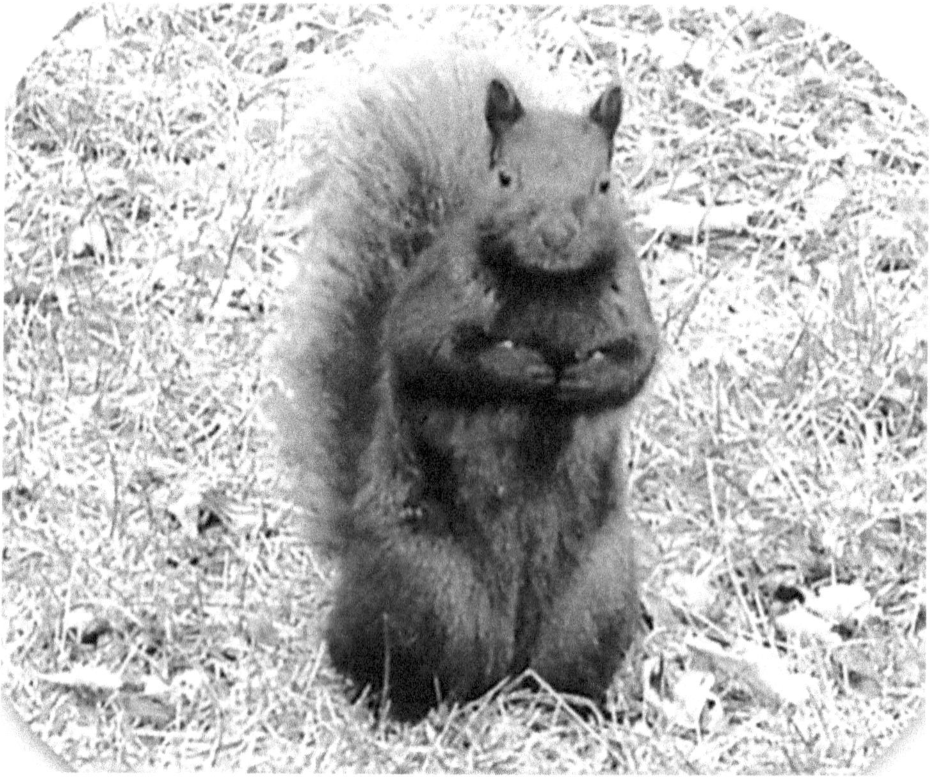

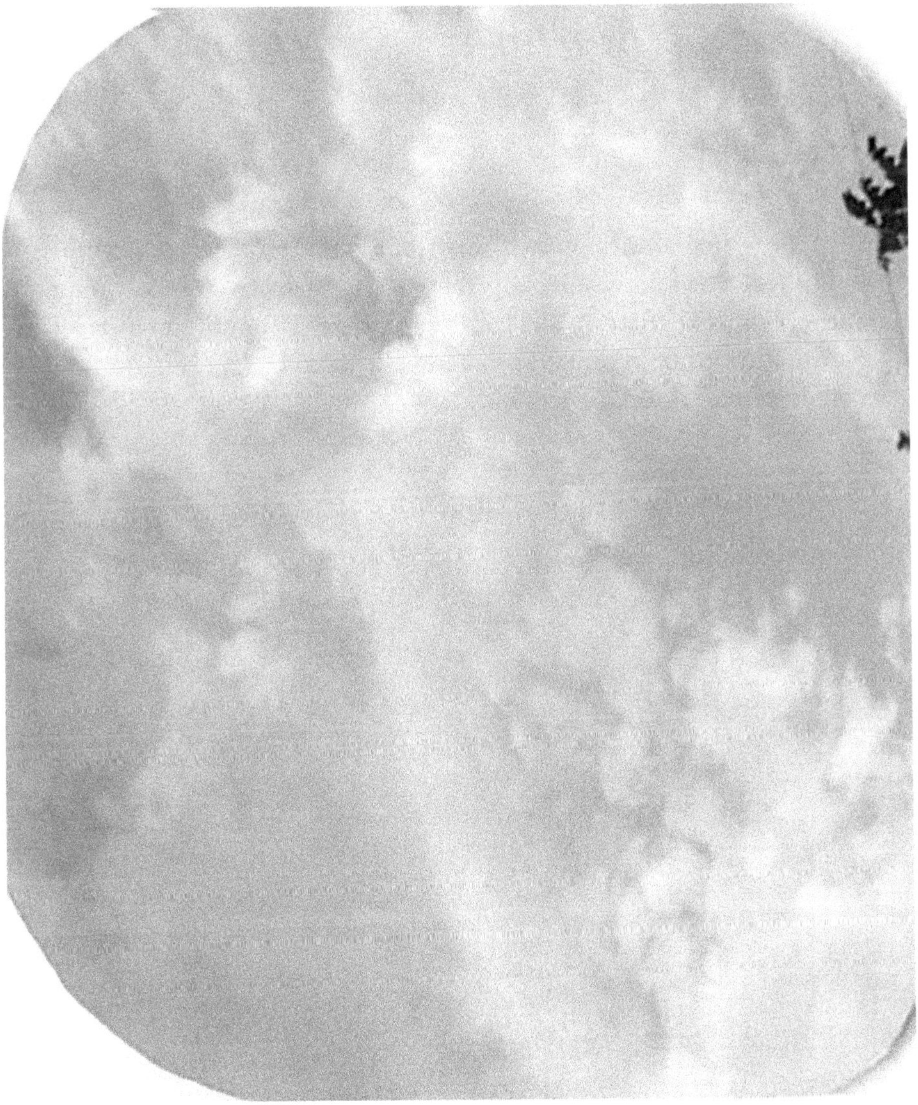

About the Author

Alice Legg had always wanted to write a book of poems and get it published. She had always hoped someone or many people would end up reading them. Alice feels that the most important part of writing this is hoping it helps someone in some way and that would make her feel so good.